TREASURE

Jemima Foxtrot is a writer, performer and theatre-maker from Yorkshire, living in Berlin. She has written and performed several critically acclaimed works for the stage including *Melody*, *Above the Mealy-mouthed Sea*, and *Pleasure Incorporated* with collaborator Lucy Allan and *Rear View* with I.O.U Theatre. She has published two collections of poetry *All Damn Day* (Burning Eye Books 2016) and *A New Game* (Burning Eye Books 2022). *Treasure* is her third book.

A New Game
(Burning Eye Books, 2022)

All Damn Day
(Burning Eye Books, 2016)

Treasure

JEMIMA FOXTROT

BAD BETTY PRESS

First published in 2024 by Bad Betty Press
Cobden Place, Cobden Chambers, Nottingham NG1 2ED

badbettypress.com

PB ISBN: 978-1-913268-58-9
EPUB ISBN: 978-1-913268-59-6

A CIP record of this book is available from the British Library.

Cover artwork by Rebecca Roscorla
Book design by Amy Acre

Printed and bound in the UK by TJ Books Limited, Padstow, Cornwall
using FSC® Certified paper from responsibly managed forests

LOTTERY FUNDED

Supported using public funding by
ARTS COUNCIL
ENGLAND

Für mein Schätzchen

CONTENTS

Treasure

I'm kindest when I give myself to a guy

go home with money in my wallet
held tight   folded firmly shimmering
myopic Irish guy   a dimple
eyes magnified through glass thick
as fingers   he's inhaling at my wetness
I'm helping him   I like to give
I'm giving him some traction
letting him make me feel good
kind American guy   good politics
he likes a drink
I like the food he buys me
we talk about public transport
has kids but doesn't discuss them
it's free in Luxemburg or something
uses the two eyes emoji when he asks me
to the sauna   he can watch
my body there on the U-Bahn
thinking about him on
me & inhaling as he touches
meat they all inhale   my
softness   I'm an experience
not made of fishnets
ponytails nail varnish lingerie
just my grubby self   smile/flesh/pelvic
floor muscles I'm pretty nodding

giving head my drunk again
grinning to myself chin up
own two nipples winking at me
from the mirror when I shed my jumpsuit
like a second skin   to piss

        pink-rimmed sight
I open my fist reveal my heart resting in it
gently thudding its subtle pumps   the joy
the horror of muteness   of numb smiles
of scrabbling for lightbulbs so
 I can glow the murky corners
timid German guy   tall rigid as God
wants to spend money on experiences
I'm an experience   sliding ready-lubed
into his DMs   hold
conversation like the woman I am
like a basket hooked in the nook
of my arm   I'm cute
did you know the longer you spend deciding
what to eat at a restaurant the less
satisfied you're likely to be with it?
hold hands as we climb the trillion
stairs to the flat with seventeen
skylights   a gin & tonic with rosemary
garnish   an unused bathtub
in the hotel room   nice things
good dinner   meat on my bones

inhale   I am kindest
when I give myself to a guy
& he pays me

Little

white flowers polka-dotting the begonia
watch me desiring the life they have
to grow under somebody's steady gaze
                         sucking my thumb
cuddle my soft toy monkey
wrapping its long arms around me
kissing its unravelling mouth
feels stupidly good
lying on my side   curled as a shrimp
like the giggling god of the babies would
& so fine   I'm a giant baby
my shower cap   my big white pants
          cry   need care like a baby too
carry me on hips forever
reaching up for the windchimes
the plastic mobiles   dreamcatchers
bury my face shyly into shoulders
at family gatherings
scared of peril in cartoons
hyenas thundering behind us
the dragon waking up

Shedding

my long lost school friends keep
killing themselves in my dreams

this time it was a girl who danced
ballet with me & laced with sweat

I gasped awake after seeing it unfold
on facebook remembering her pink

eczema her personal hill too steep
& the net weaved insufficiently

the two dogs howled at 3am
either at some invisible threat

or in a visceral funeral tribute
the living tell me it's a sign

of loneliness or growing up
or of my own damp survival

but I just want it to stop
tell my unconscious again

that suicide's not funny
& there's not many of us left

Oak

bleached morning after our first date
sap & seeds   ketchup und mayo
you're an oak tree   it's obvious
clung to you keenly   like baby pink
clematis   auf der schmutzigen Straße
mit Pommes   vomiting & you're sorry
for me   those worried eyes as patches
of sky   you even kiss my sicky mouth
those scalloped giving leaves   dub me
little hippy   I don't deny for a second
I'm a treehugger   & the name sticks
so next time   your branches seek me
high in bed   inhale your acorn breath
earlier tonight   you held my feet down
with your feet beneath the laden table
cooked too many florets of soggy sorry
broccoli slid into the kitchen bin but
I was rooted in our second date forest
mein Lieblingsbaum   meine Eiche

It's the biggest marketing scam in the world

that straight men don't like to talk
they can't do it
to each other   seems gay or something
can only do it to you
someone bred from childhood to listen
that's me
let them spunk themselves out
they've found a post they can hitch their experience to
a bollard with excellent tits
pixelated   ugly
still worth half a month's rent
I might as well cum
in the post for these people
I might as well let them fill me with air
      listen as they pass me
            their ugly splintered bits
& what's the difference
between that & O I DON'T KNOW
listening to another day's news
it's nice to hear what it's like to have money

the platypus of chance

is living in my wardrobe   nestled in party dresses fallen off their hangers
beak broad & shovellike   a speculum splitting open a comedy swag bag
of cash   avalanche of gold coins   rapunzel's plaited braid unspooling
down the tower *you have to snatch the work up while it exists* she purrs
at me   she's the platypus of chance   & so she's always after money
platypuses have two layers of skin & carry air in between as insulation
cash as bubble wrap   gross paper money bundles everything up tight
the platypus's fur is sleek as if newly conditioned with the fancy stuff
platypuses glow under UV light & the males   in heat   are venomous
after hatching an egg   she checks on her puggle   still with the shell
on his head & I expect a colony soon   beavertails batting my sequins
my denim they'll be flexing in their tiny leather driving gloves saying
come grab this crown & this wheel too & this one & this one & this one

going going going

I shouted at her for not understanding   my whole work
my whole self   the rightness of this she used to be an expert
in me or in what I was doing   now i'm blurred as august
she only sees a splodge   can't process my new-me haircut
my shifted perspective   she doesn't understand my reason
for being any longer & so that's my excuse for losing it too
our future as an ugly ball of gluey grime picked up from past
for not recognising my flashcards scrawled in blunt crayon
exponentially more desperate   saying *understand me listen*
tried semaphore tried morse binary code   going   one thing
affects another & another so *listen to me*   going going going
understand me   going going *remember me*   *remember me*

done right

ballet teacher complimented my rond de jambe
I almost died of joy
ballet teacher called me miss green because
my sweaty green striped top
felt like a real dancer then I did   sipped my water
stretched inexpertly
safe in the knowledge I circle my straight leg correctly
despite my mismatched socks
despite my faded leggings with a hole in the crotch
I text u in the break
we joke our new joke about praise kinks
but everyone likes   surely
everyone likes to be told that they're doing it right

after & outside   I'm once again a caterpillar
face rimmed with frost
like salt like ket   like stopping saying yes
the city's lit-up kitchen windows
smug with yellow heat & nearly Christmas
my sleepy carcass
its sputtering spark inside
clambers on the bike

once upon a time   I was a lemon rind
I won the competition
of losing a man who was bad for me

& the prize
was a million cigarettes
for weeks after
gusts of not good enough
hissed everywhere from
vents in the pavement

on the battered laptop-telly at finally home
it's snowing too
the characters on an unseasonal wine tour
the vineyard's bare grids
the undone sudoku
a new year looms
I text again
tell u how I once was lemon rind

u tell me i'm a clever girl
u tell me that it's all ok
u tell me that I did it right

bad trip

it's only moss pushing
between your toes love
the spores aren't people
moss is brainless honest

concentrate harder on
each strand of grass as magic
the outside's not a battle
but if it were we could
let it win   shit ok   no

squeeze this tangerine
hard as you need
we weren't going to eat it anyway
food goes nowhere in your body
stomach's a boarded-up shop
     when you're high like us

don't imagine not having someone
to pour love into   you've got me
i'm here pretty baby   yes yes yes
sweetie   that's right i've got you breathe

but words are all made up
if you think about it
scaffolding we hang actions from
shit ok   no

perhaps listen to a podcast
close your eyes
cut out visual stimuli
remember swimming
in whitley bay? yes?
the freezing hug of sea

o I slept so   wow   like I was dead   o wow   still as whitby jet
   duckling feathers   down-covered tongue   so sleep is a kind
of kindness   wow   to myself   my vision pigmented   inside
of a circus tent   opened my eyes   saw the world in stripes   fat
   bands   of happiness rollered on & o not lonely
under my hospital duvet   guilt-free   silently singing inside myself
   o the best nap of my life   o spilled water evaporating into
   chequerboard air   deader than I've ever slept   soaking
in the artificial night   dark-chocolate corduroy   my insides
on a flatscreen   wow   on wheels   the expected tiny black lumps
   they covered me in orange stuff & puffed me up with air
   & o I slept like snow white   though I must've looked
an oompa loompa   while they twiddled their scalpels   I climbed
into a bath of bisto   sunk into a plunge pool of custard   gunky
   but worried about absolutely nothing   nurse tells me I'm
   not crazy   that I didn't imagine the pain   in her kind voice
      says *soon you'll be home with all the tubes taken out*
in my tight-fitting tortoiseshell   with my hobbies & interests
my houseplants   their chlorophyll fingers   my health as a prize
      I snatched back   o but wow I'll miss that anaesthetic

that nap

so here it is

we rub ourselves together & kiss as if
we're maddening   she eats me sliding
off the sofa   my body puddled butter
her jacket black as a butler's   her hair
as Cruella de Vil best of both lets me
drink my wine only if I'm good   says
she's just getting started   wishes she
could make money like I do but hates
dick   dating women is terrible too
their glossiness drama   their bubbles
of shimmer she wants the next poetry
night she sees me at to feature a poem
about her   so here it is   she paints
two-metre canvases of owl eyes staring
but art doesn't work when you try to
make it about something   she is a
heavy-lidded pleasure   wants to snort
ritalin off my belly I let her   no cash
changes hands   I imagine I have her
to talk to each day laugh at my clients
their stupidity   how I take their euros
how I leave right after they cum on me
I imagine going home to her   kissing
the abstract tattoo above her left breast
its latticing its fadedness & the night is
broken as the sky turns light & I know
now I'm here at the enchanted part

treasure

the lake is treasure

lying back &   smelling it   letting my bodyfat carry me   thankful

the water–snake wriggling the surface treasure

she changed my whole sexuality with a sideways hug treasure   turned me briefly into a peach

                    glowing jewelled reward   treasure

the way she monkeys me she's that celery green

reassure me   treasure   & I picked those raspberries the colour of her nipples little treasure in my palm   the best I've ever touched   drupelets between

tongue & ridged roof of mouth

my time alone treasured   the sticks we brought back from hiking   a memory of blushing at a text

that he sent me   foolish treasure   when he called me his girl

she says it's a mixture of the patriarchy & hormones that lets me fall in love with lampposts

& it is   I'm treasure   my body floating on the lake

warm treasure   treasure of wet   lying back & smelling it

Ingo & the pine trees

communicate   root to root

if my finger gets snipped   my bark bleeds

> *pass the drinks around*
>
> *make sure everyone's hydrated*

they know   mostly   when to bud

I wish I was a   no I don't   a tree

> *slow & somehow imaginary*

give a baby sapling a chance

they do   they protect them

> *let's not talk about the things we need*

there's a tree in the park that's a clownfish

one real lover has one big mole on his ribs

sideways-looking cyclops

he's my secondary-school boyfriend but stretched out

> *slowly imagined*

over time   his branches gorgeous-tangled

snapping   twigs blunted from decades of testing them

butterfly thumbnut ears

> *he knows   mostly   when to bud*

the pine trees that circle this city boast perfect teeth

present game shows

they grow in dry soil   don't ask for much

& their needles must have really wanted me

otherwise they wouldn't have entered

my dreams   a stream that dribbles first

then widens into sea

otherwise that pine tree

wouldn't have fucked me like a heart-attack

otherwise that pine tree

christ I'm pathetic

licking my phone screen with that photo

of that tree on it

there's a tree in the park that's a dragonfly

otherwise that pine tree

wouldn't have showed me its bitter belly

graffitied with initials of teenagers

& told me that it hurt

but in a good slow way

pass the drinks around

make sure everyone's hydrated

I hate the way my reptile brain

wants a baby

my reptile brain smart as a rock

a baby

with a stranger

or a man with great taste

a tree with mental health problems

a drug problem

a tree with a messy flat

& pint glasses full of chopsticks

on every available surface

a tree who puts his headphones

on me as he kisses me in the laundrette

tree says   *I love your eyes*

                                 your   tits ass   curly hair

                                 your pale pink lips

& lust is such

dumb sugar   revving everything up

lust is nectarines & when it happens

I'm feeling the same

foreign coins in my pocket

can't remember quite which one's which

just his lips pressed to mine in hello

& goodbye

his bark spinning round

in the tumble dryer

sad sun

feels like a failure for boomeranging home grown up
but sun was shot in both legs by soldiers   wants to hide
& watch the outside world roll by   saddening frankly

gentle boy sun painted activism on for the day & paid
for it   dim little sun had an eye shoved down his throat
& they still couldn't work out what the problem was

sun's got a slipped disk   can't pull himself up by his bootstraps
seen too much   that's nothing   perhaps it's genetic depression
neckless sun   couldn't escape bed to walk around the corner

where an unseasonal ice cream van sat   its engine running
its mr whippies calling & the flame red tree outside the window
announced that another year had happened fast without him

Courage

for Bridget & Josie

where would we be without each other to read
& redraft the difficult messages
to men   like me saying
this one won't be a freebie
I'll have to give more work & time
we wouldn't be lounging in bravery's glow the way
we are now
or like you saying
you not turning up to my show
being incommunicado   hurt me
we wouldn't be expressing
our young boundaries like good bold girls
like hammers   like humans
with real pebble bendable vertebrae
or you saying
no
you don't know how to make me cum
someone told us
we should perform a ceremony
in the crook of the new moon
carve a word into a long candle
mine was pale pink like my cotton bedding
& burn it every night
the word we chose was courage

Missus

we're in that early phase
playacting as your hausfrau
flushes me peach with sex

if you'd let me wash
your socks by hand
I would

so enjoy me doing dishes
'til the hot runs out
& pray it never does

Das Konzert

slide past each other   well–oiled
into wide aisles
dance in all the thoughts
the music spawns
the thrumming oyster shell
its peaks stiffened with organic glue
        blend of urgency
& energy & kindness

our bikes ride funny
when we step out
of the gig
the moon's a scrunched receipt
the architecture held us
in its stiff yet giving grip
& my attention's resculpted
horns stuck on & warts shaved off
& that's the point of art isn't it?
& isn't art the whole fucking point?

cum at all costs

I'm playing mother nature in monmouth
    two hundred a day   to accost strangers
dress dyed naturally with beetroots avocado pits
    mother nature   eating chips & curry sauce
cross-legged on the pavement   middle finger to passersby
tut   my polystyrene tray   *it's a climate festival*
mother nature on a rager   before she flew here
cadging fags outside the späti at 3am   standard
    ran to Berlin   like all the other stupid peter pans
their black techno cosplay   my valley hometown flooded
again   sandbags spill their innards   her
or is it my   ruptured gut   healing slower than
 expected   offers herself sliced up   my make-up run off
    like all the other stupid hookers
she's porn-choked   her body turns
chucking up my chips & curry   in the square
grabs her apricot breasts   on a memorial bench
in memory of our childhood   everyone's watching
puts her fingers up myself   checks we're still there
        we sniff them & it's not good news
my mate was a freelance apocalypse
    different event   great casting
he was a guaranteed good time   the death cult kind
arrived at the soupy-aired club   hoping to get his dick wet

his misplaced swagger   spilled a beer
on a woman's sequined shoulder   wore tight jeans
& cherry red converse   explained his tattoos in detail
to blinkless eyes   the honeybee   the spider
the native American chief   he covered that one up eventually
      a woman he was fucking   ok me
told him it wasn't ok   a crudely-drawn medusa
      frowned as he clenched his left pec
his consonants slipping
   unsubtly took women to the bathroom
promised it was just for drugs
            but unzipped himself immediately
& I slid into the cubicle with him & my gay
best friend *my bodyguard*   apocalypse was generous
racked up on the cistern
   offered everyone a plastic straw
needed to cum at all costs   as apocalypse does
after everyone was done & home time texted
mother nature went back with him
& mimed to my friend that she'd call

visiting the visiting business

always take a book with you
if you're there before them   you should
be reading it when they arrive
men are stupid   no not all men
it blows their minds
that you a mere woman   a simple cottage prostitute
might be clever enough
to read a book
you're like a talking chipmunk
they don't read them
too busy sending emails
making calls
with their bluetooth headsets   like dickheads
if they go to the toilet
be reading the book   phone away
when they get back
for extra points
make it a classic   *Anna Karenina*
something they've heard of
but not something you
should have necessarily read already
google the politics of the
country they're from
beforehand & tell
them the job they do
is morally reprehensible

assuming it is   it probably is
they'll like that
they'll smile & say
I know but I love it
their catlike smarm
consume everything they offer
they don't like vegans
they want simplicity
not a fusspot with requirements
tuck into your steak with vigour
its tender expense

a poem celebrating tabletop

because you love building worlds inside   when I
catch you at it   I smile like warmed milkor as a
daisy chain does   our outdoor lives are workaday
envelopes spawning admin   our energy in the red
forget myself then   sitting at your painting table
gripping the brush   willing dexterity's safe birth
hope to stay in the lines with the nerves of a teenager
i'm groping for compliments   *a strong first try*   tell me
just stay calm   rinse your brushes   choose weapons
keep going until you have your army for frostgrave
locked in the anglepoise light   yoghurt pot terrain
mini landscape   &   remember what tiktok said   *it's the*
nerds   these guys aint stepping out on you after *kings*
of war   they will hold you tight as the fleshy human
prize you are & true you act as if your life has been a
quest that's led to me   so I'm constant now as the
ridicule you've lived with   & stuck to your guns
sexy doesn't cover it   watching you camouflage new
turtles into the scene & a dainty green crowned frog
using it as bait   or target   & when I find you so
very concentrated I bless my new topography   the
way you show your love   by infodump   all your
extravagant fantasies   tiny double chin   breath held
your seriousness   as you pupil your soldier's eye
zen as a just closed window   the middle of July

undercovers

the neighbours' sex blares strong
through the bubble thin ceiling
unsurprising urban evening lovesong
I briefly invite my fingers along
it doesn't work & I'm lonely

& I sleep but it doesn't stop
my utter love for world
& its repetitive adventure
the way I wake up every morning
& it's all at once the future   new books
the same four walls   mugs of milky tea
the day stretching out like a mystery
solved as I don't get dressed & eat
a sharing bag of crisps for breakfast

the tenacious regret over wasting time
sticks around like a bruise or a love bite
journey shouldn't stop when I get home
explore the inner workings of my time alone
slice a chunk of the mountain of my life off
every day & spread it as a lump of butter
& yes the mountain's ever shrinking down
but everything gets coated   greasy & delicious

long beans

negotiate it first before you asphyxiate me
so yes I like it but you don't know that yes
I mean yet   push my back down
until my torso lies flat on the table

for dinner   you're in charge until I am
choose the restaurant   choose the food
deny me & let me sit on you   make me touch
the parts of me that feel good & then don't
let me do it anymore   give me those broad
green notes   long beans   seaweed
know I'll change them into groceries
into generosity
to my friends with less   it's magic
I turned them
into lychees from the posh organic shop
                into the walls that keep the wind out
negotiate it with me before
                we start playing   before we
start pretending you don't respect me
I'm on the bedroom floor & begging you again
                you say you don't want more mess
my period is visiting & blood's all over
it's like a horror film in here   I joke
I just want you to grab at me
you can cover my mouth up   hold my nose
first you have to ask me

Regent's Park

I watched a pelican eating a pigeon whole
saw how it struggled in the grim sack of beak
    saw it flap as an unravelling secret
    saw denial   for a second   in the dim black eyes
my naysayers say I'm making that part up   i'm not
its diseased feet that made it hobble
       & everyone's upset now
       apart from the guy who shrugs & says
       animal kingdom
       there's always a guy who says that

the cauldron

the cauldron contains body parts
placentas & driftwood in a urine soup
I add to it each tepid day as I scroll
as I sort out my psychic trash

mouse crawls up to it & out of itself
leaves its pelt on the ground & proceeds
his skeleton caging the greasy jellybean
organs   limps up to the lip   takes one
look behind him then dives right in
 bye bye mousey   see you never

the cauldron is full of my gusto
& bluster   my failure & dirty nails
my   women & I make everything
possible   we chant & flash
our emerald teeth
we sing punk out of our navels
& lick the ground & scream
the constant disappointment
of rarely finding fairness
the best petrol there is

the cauldron holds all my years
of spittle & grit collected
in the bottom of beer cans
my hardness exists in the cauldron
& it bobs like a rotten egg

Orgasm

every time it's close
think his thick fingers
pale pink nails & thumbpad
visiting through the bars
the silver argos bunk-bed
fleshy spider   impatient
I stop   adjust the laptop
& then always again
in the second before
the wave might break
think archaic punishments
paunchy crawling insect hand
chopped off   disposed of
rotting down in an allotment
breaking up in compost to
grow rhubarb garden peas
broad beans   cabbages or
raspberries climbing canes
imagine a seagull snatching
his slowly mouldering digits
from the blood-nourished soil
its evil yellow beak & then he
might stop his fiddling finally
might nip it in the overblown
& ugly bud   I wheel up over
back gardens my seagull view
on all that's still growing

I'm saying it

you're standing at the serving hatch
big dumb grin   pretty steaming pillows
of restorative dumplings   held in front of you
        a cracked & patterned plate
bowl ladle-filled to the brim with broth

i'm trying to catch the letters that chase through
our rafters like palm squirrels   that wriggle like
the maggots in your uncle's treacle tin for fishing

you're standing at the diner door
big dumb grin   the neon light
spelling our names in pink & flickering cursive
you beckon me inside   fluffy hair & puppylike
i was waiting for a chair
to build itself beneath me
i didn't think it could
yet here you are all made of wood
the pages of my notebook
are overcooked slices of my heart
at the carvery   the letters settle down now
congregate in a line on the handrail of our steps
ok there   I'm saying it baby
        I love you

Nice is different from good

after Stephen Sondheim

I asked for the best room they had and they gave me this shit
bigger than my flat   he came quicker than frying an egg
then we slept   an extra two hundred for that
            red wine headache beginning its lichen creep
got turned away at breakfast for not knowing the last name
rookie error
walk of shame in my tiny black dress
put on woollen gloves from the Euro shop
            but I know things now
he said *whatever you might say against him*
Hitler was a great leader   unsurprising perhaps given
he makes companies more efficient
he got the job done
you can judge me for opening my body to a Nazi apologist
sometimes you have to cut away the excess fat
but if it wasn't me it would be someone else
& he prides himself on being gentlemanly
sickening grin   eyes bulging like a cartoon wolf
I take myself   through cold blue morning
all the way home on the U

Hawthorn

radio woke me up to tell me about the tree of the year
as selected from nominations   submitted by the public

strength no actually   *resilience* that's what she said
I had   & true   I guess   I've needed it

tree rooted down into cockleshell beach grew wonky
for self-preservation leaning into the vinegar wind

but let's not celebrate mere survival   let's cosy up
to how I thrive   magnify my bark my stretchmarks

the tree's nominator has photos stuck to his fridge
generations of family sitting in its anchored arms

I hold my leaves open to the raggedy sky
tell the wind it can mould me   I don't care

yes   its nominator named it   *a lovely little tree*
he & the presenter both marvelled at its hardiness

he kept talking & talking   this tree lover
eventually they faded him out for the sport

Kinderwunsch

my biggest fear is miscarriage
I'd told you on the phone
perhaps not strictly true but
I just don't know how I'd cope
sometimes   I'm sure I should
retrain as a midwife like Laura
an umpire passing pebbles from
one pocket to another & I come
to your mother with a five kilo
cake in my hands to convince
her I'm sumptuous & fertile
pink apple conker english rose
I laid seventeen eggs for the cake
zested my own lemons & dug my
own distress whipped cream until
the world changed ate strawberries
to celebrate   carried it all the way
on the train to prove I might be
fatter & full of milk one day
I just don't know how I'd cope
the heavy french red casserole pot
left out on the stovetop for all to see

The Sterile West

the only time I ever get to the west of the city is
to visit the men who pay me to have sex with them
 o but yes I went to a dentist there once   cried
in the chair because she was so kind in her gleaming
coat   brighter than my teeth   speaking to me in
English   trying to make the whole sorry scenario cheap
as possible   she must have sensed I needed it   perhaps
because of the holes in my jumper   maybe I subconsciously
went there looking poor   I thought about my future
as she measured the gaps between my   teeth
 for a retainer   & now it's all over I'm a film star
with tannin stains   eight years in London
 taught me to think of cities as existing north & south
of the river   the laziness of crossing as palpable as lack
        I cross the Spree to my boyfriend's flat
 an old contract   he needs to hold on to
  everyone here holds on to what they have
because everything's so hard to get   one day I want
to put our kids in it   I've hinted this to him
& he takes it like a champ   he knows what I do for cash
texts me that he loves me before & after wants to know
I'm safe   says he needs me   it's nice to feel needed
not just wanted   nice to feel him at my back as I stir
 the pasta sauce   stroking my comedowns   offering

T-shirts to sleep in   nice gets a bad rep
     for me it's egg yolk
contentment   feather duvets mostly they're visiting
on business   the hotels in the west   red blocks
 on dark blue   in Charlottenburg at an expensive
Japanese restaurant I sit behind a slab of raw tuna
plump & dark   imagine an elf's liver   green rosette
of wasabi an evil eye   the most delicious thing
    make cheery conversation because my rent
depends on it   In Tempelhof   I spend my earnings
 in Woolworth   a stick blender   a clock &   buy a börek
from the market stall gone up by 50c like everything
 I love how the grease makes the bag translucent
makes the extra money worth it   grease is healing
Kreuzberg   at my cube of flat look into my
low slung mirror   hung especially for me & worry
in that ugly way we do   I'm getting too fat too
 old & round to keep doing this but still not sagging
 stay thankful for something   in Mitte
I pick up Sofia from her private school
 for 12 an hour tell her she needs to practise her flute
in Lichtenberg   I smoke weed with my boyfriend
talk politics in the kitchen   visit Rosa Luxemburg
in her grave & thank her for all she did   o but yes
 once I went to a play in the west   actually   yes
     with a visiting friend   about climate collapse
& we ate chinese dumplings & aubergines

with minced pork afterwards & the waitress was
so kind in her tabard   more maroon
than I bleed
I try to look presentable   only so much I can
take the piss   but the sterile west is unheimlich
        & I was born to sully it

Großbuchstabenliebe

now I've met a german man
who's trying to understand me
I capitalise Nouns sometimes as if for him
& who do I think I am eating my Gyoza
with Vinegar & Notebook at the Table
bumper Bunch of Daffodils sparking
trapped inside this wirklich rainy Spring
writing my Poetry like somebody cares
strange to think now that somebody does
finally somebody's fallen in Love
catch my little round Face peering cutely
back out from the barely used Mirror
tarnished Moon   corrupt Cherub
eventually witnessed   so pretty

Toddling
after Sylvia Plath

funeralaic   scariest on two feet
hands in the earth & sunburnt
sealed like a letter   a determined
two fingers to my petty dim life
expanding yourself as explosions
quieting your bang   as guns do
you're eloquent as a euphonium
adding to my actions with oompah
o bottomfeeder my marmite guess
constant as rain   boxes of tampons
closer somehow than my local pub
adulthood proper my precious tie
loud as coughs in the kino   in life
as a kite in the bulbous mountain sky
a bowl of porridge all humble comfort
solid as our gross & lingering dreams
wrong as an unacknowledged sadness
forever imagined   still never your face

red brick like you

your name is the water you swim through
body's disconnected from brain most days
gives that comedy *argh* of pain as you move
& the weather erratic as unexplained violence
we exist inside its dome firmly count the days
the glaciers melt in a panic clutching damp
handkerchiefs to their chests & shrieking
we have to make the best of it
you unuprootable stem-filled dandelion sap
make your decisions once & stick to them
blonde labrador giant tortoise whale elephant
i'm your decision & can barely believe my luck
& the socialist monument we visit is red brick
like you   it's far too warm for new year's day
i'm sweating through my jumper my puffer
so everyone nods us their acknowledgments
that we're nearing the end of our liveable earth
the travelling birds scatter back to us early
& the crocuses confused are already singing

Lemonade

a triolet for my friends

I want my life   its pith & skin
its drunken kitchen table song
friends say *love you Mim come in*
popping bottles juicing grins
my love for life was ugly thin
but now the grey is glimmering
I'm sure it isn't wrong
I want my life   its pith & skin
its drunken kitchen table song

Superman

never thought I'd ride in a Porsche   let alone
make out in one
make out like I like it   make like I'm impressed
          one glass of sweet wine sunk through my body
 weight sliding into my gaps   chardonnay's back
in fashion
if it's made from grapes   I'll drink it
I drank it   he didn't   he was driving
his low Porsche home
gave me a cigarette as if it was a biscuit & smoked
so I do too
          left my battered old music
on his low leather seat the colour of cow embryos
or cappuccinos or devonshire clotted cream fudge
into a garage that tetrises men's sports cars into place
his hand on my thigh   matter of fact   hard to get
out of
see his frowning working frowning wrinkles deep
when he was very   he didn't say   how young
a thirty-nine year old woman showed him what to do
how her body worked   *got good grounding*   good
grooming
then he was off   naught to sixty
   left his unsullied music in her grown up bed   keeps
interrupting me
 wants the Superman symbol tattooed on his chest
      for his work saving orphans in his shitty shiny suit

he's contracted a garden-variety saviour complex
& there's nothing I can do
but I just want him to pay my rent   buy me
a better bike

              buy me new speakers   headphones
cappuccinos
there's suddenly so much I need
buy me chardonnay   & veal   some shiny new music
want him to buy me buy me buy me

New Bike

swift one two tells me I met the curb
successfully   Will said I should look
at the gap I need to go through   big
brothers telling me I should look at the
ball I need to catch   beach french cricket
stating the obvious   mouldering leaves
copper moon   I never had good fingers
cack-handed *you know Jemima can't*
butter bread?   so watch me now as
like calligraphy   I weave through bollards
rizla sleek monster pressed up between
my legs & a bicycle is a perfect thing   pedal
& create inner discos   last night I glided
through near dead streets at midnight
& grabbed   my childhood back
with both hands on the handlebars
this machine speaks to me of everything
I lost   so now I'm a lioness who's practical
she sleeps when she needs to   hunts when
she has to   she takes the streets as fast
as danger   so far always gets home safe

when I board my Ryanair flight to Manchester

I smooth my monkey tail all up my back
                    tuck it safe under my collar
                    hook its tip behind the highschool tie
                    I wore especially for homecoming
I daub on lack of anxiety
          ready to fly
try an extra smile with the stewardess
enjoy watching her garnet lipstick stretch
     remember it from last time
buy the vacuum-packed olives
pop one every ten minutes
until we land & &
& home is a rope-ladder
its blister-giving rungs
the full pie dishes
the picnics that mean family
swim-scurry down Market Street
the train across to Yorkshire
sop up its gravy landscape
step off it & I'm naked
streaking   tail flapping wildly
          my slew of flaws & all
 a smirk at my new authenticity
back into Mytholmroyd's jaws

Untying

what is pink & knotted? my busy hands   my mischief
my craving for a baby   the knot of friends that changed
or the knot of them I slipped from   fibres fraying
from the rope
knot of cords in the bottom drawer that charge nothing
I misread unites as unties all the time
& I was the one who left
knot of mussels in the white wine pot   unlocking
their bodies
willing me to eat them while I pretend to be something
i'm not   my knotted stomach as I wait for the results
the rotten knot of my constant performance
community unties around stabbing
the little knot of trees in the motorway's central bank
ice cube exploding when it hit my chest thanks to the
knot of air at its core   it was a wonderful weekend
again
all knotted up with nothing
& for that i dredge up thanks
suffering unties us all!
i can untie fuck all
despite how hard I try
damp human cord cut & knotted
angry little dog knotted up outside Tesco
but we're tied to each other & liking it
me   a sunburned sailor
you   a pale & muscular diver up

for eventual air from under the week
workers of the world untie!
the knots in our accounts paying our rent
your money every month

Mim

I step inside her   shabby glistered garter
she's broke like me of course but classier

laughs more   I hope not in a vulgar way
she just titters pink & keenly at his jokes

hält ihre Klappe über the box of clothes
I found on the street & wore without washing

keeps it shut about most politics too
she's free from my persistent trickle of shame

she knows what she wants it's not complicated
Ich will Geld she says & holds out her hands

piggy bank with fingernails cut close & cleaned
she smiles as she says it's the oldest profession

she keeps my tall boyfriend's existence a secret
his tenderness a bonbon reserved for only me

a client says the rich-man-top-hat
-tyrant image is way out of date

mim & me   we nod   agree
me & mim   we're not so sure

ich hab Lust

for pancakes with limes & brown sugar   for the mystery
dog who dreams at my feet   for the shapes you & I
will make together as yet unspecified but I know
one's a wind-filled sail   lust for pushing my tongue
through pitted black olives   you handing over your
crackling   for bonfires in imagined or remembered
back gardens   for the decision tree that grew & got me
here   that tree that blossoms & sheds & bends
for hearing the church bells hammer themselves silly
from my fresh made bed   ich hab Lust auf deinen Kuss
baby   your silly songs & microdancing   & those
plastic wipe down polkadot tablecloths sold in rolls
outside everything shops & for women's bikini strings
I've got lust for swimming my life away   for loving
every hopeful snot-nosed child the same   for pistachio
ice cream in a paper cup & getting sweaty from the
trashy summer sun & a large pilsner & nasty sex
& waking up to the sea's bright sound & cheap holidays
with friends & forgetting all the men who treated me
badly & painting the kitchen with you baby my shackles
shrugged off at my feet

Church

genuflected   aching knees   & narrow french pew
cross myself to see how it feels   my fingers as
   somebody else's
watch the candles & wonder who I'd light one for
my maternal grandma   I think she'd approve
religion's been cruel to people like us
           the darkwood sluts   the good time girls
but god as my witness
some of us   we're just trying to wrangle our power
back from the species that took it
& it works sometimes   feels good
like my pain one day
           started printing money
& I've come out to bask
 in the last of the languageless light
remember my blonde twenties
how life curls sweet around itself
eyes pointed sideways in photographs
my body stretching to remember
one cell at a time   what it was like
 what freedom was
before any of the sour stuff   that began at age ten
a cruel God standing at the starting block
is a master that nobody chooses
it's just something that some of us get

pretty little fish

honey   this week I am a hummingbird
don't try to hold me   cheetah-spotted
quick as summer slipping by   this week
darling I'm lonely as the clocktower
I sip my negroni & clang
puncture clouds with my own jokes
this week I'm tall & my trousers fit
latex-tight   I still look good
I've been cooking endless spaghetti
this week & using it to scaffold life
the photo of emma mica & me
keeps shining from my desk this
week in the accumulating chaos
this week I can say no
this week I am a ficus tree
a sunshine mango smoothie
an animated elephant   no
this week I am a pretty little fish
swimming for my own sweet sake

Acknowledgements

Thanks to the *FU Review*, where a version of 'that nap' was originally published.

I'd like to thank Bad Betty Press for believing in this book's potential from the very beginning. The biggest thank you possible goes to Amy Acre for being so precise, diligent and kind in her role as editor and for being oh so wise. You have truly been the best editor I could have asked for.

Thank you to Joey Connolly, as always, for being my poetry sounding board and guiding light. I always know I've done a good job when you like it. Your unwavering belief in me is a big part of what lets me do this.

A huge and warm thanks to Rebecca Roscorla for letting us use her image for the cover and to Sam Ratcliffe for finding and suggesting it. Thanks to Jungle Tide, Sri Lanka for providing an unofficial writing retreat where a good chunk of this book was written and refined.

Thank you to all of my friends, always, and specifically to Bridget, Sam, Maja, Mica, Emma, and Olivia who helped me on this journey.

And finally a huge thanks to the man to whom this book is dedicated, who sees my sparkle, takes me as I am, and cares for me so wonderfully. I love you Flo.